D.I.Y. Bookkeeping

Valerie Johnston

Owner of Profit Meadow Bookkeeping

ISBN: 9781093390834.

Disclaimer: Do not mistake this book for proper legal/CPA advice. I am a bookkeeper trained to keep books and do taxes, but I am not a CPA and have no way of knowing your personal situation through a book. This book is written to a large audience, and cannot be everything to everyone. Nevertheless, it will give you the framework to make you more prepared when you go to do your taxes. In addition, all of the names, locations, businesses, and situations in this book are fictional and purely for educational purposes.

DEDICATION

This book is dedicated to my Babes, Junebug, and Buddy. Babes, thank you for believing in me and this business, before I even made a dime. Junebug and Buddy, thanks for napping so quietly and sweetly so Mommy could write this book. :)

1. I'm Glad You're Here!

You've started your own business!! Congratulations!! You get to do the things you love, and make money while doing them!! You're free!!

Well... almost. Unfortunately, you still have to do some of the things you don't like to do, like marketing, branding, and... bookkeeping.

I imagine that you're reading this book because you can't afford a bookkeeper right now, but you realize the importance of keeping your books straight. I'm so impressed that you are taking the time to get things right the first time! Most business owners just ignore their numbers until they can afford someone, but not you!! You're proactive! You're brave! You're freaking awesome!

I'm going to teach you the simplest way to categorize your income/expenses. Anyone can do it!

And when your business starts to boom, and you simply don't have the time to do it yourself anymore, you can give me a call! :)

As most of the people I market to have a Sole Proprietorship or a single-member LLC, this book will be written toward those entities. However, the information is transferable. If you have a specific question about your entity (S-corp, C-corp, Nonprofit, etc.) email me at valerie@profitmeadow.com. I'll be glad to help! :)

2. The Accounting Equation and Double-Entry Bookkeeping

Don't let the chapter heading scare you away! We're going to go slowly, and you can always contact me with any questions! :)

The Accounting Equation is this: Assets = Liabilities + Equity.

Assets are what you own. Most of the time, assets are tangible, physical items, like cash, cars, land, and equipment. Intangible assets can also exist, like a business's logo.

Liabilities are what you owe other people, like a credit card, payroll taxes that haven't been paid yet, or a loan. Some of the time, you take out a liability in order to obtain an asset (like taking out a loan to buy a house.)

Equity is the value of the difference between your assets and your liabilities.

For example, you want to purchase a house for $100,000. You make a down payment of $30,000 and get a loan for $70,000.

Asset ($100,000) = Liabilities ($70,000) + Equity ($30,000)

If you make a payment of $10,000 toward the capital of the loan (let's not consider interest right now) the equation would now look like this:

Asset ($100,000) = Liabilities ($60,000) + Equity ($40,000)

And THAT is double-entry bookkeeping!

Double-entry means that if something affects one category, then another category is going to be affected as well.

For example, if you gain an asset, then you're going to gain either a liability, equity, or both!

If you make a sale in your business, money is going into your checking account (an asset) and you are going to have more equity in the business!

If you purchase items to sell, money is going out of your checking account (an asset) and you are going to have less equity in the business!

If you make a purchase with your credit card (a liability) you are going to have less equity in the business as well.

There are millions of examples, but here are some key principles to keep in mind:

*Just because two categories are affected doesn't mean that they can't be on the same side of the equation. You can increase one asset while decreasing another. You can increase a liability while decreasing equity.

*No matter what, two categories are ALWAYS affected.

Now, what are these categories that I'm speaking of? They are called the Chart of Accounts. Go ahead and go to the next chapter, and I'll explain these categories in a more practical way.

(For more on double-entry bookkeeping, you can see Chapter 10, where I dive in to Debits and Credits. As a bookkeeper, you MUST understand debits and credits, which is how the bookkeeping software works. However, I managed to write this book without mentioning them, so it isn't crucial for the practical business owner to know. You can do your own bookkeeping without this knowledge. I simply wanted to make this information available to you if you find yourself asking "Why?" to anything that I'm doing in the following chapters. If you're not a numbers person, and you are just trying to get by, ignore Chapter 10.)

3. THE CHART OF ACCOUNTS

Karen owns Quilt Me One Too, where she makes and sells her handmade quilts. It started out as a simple side business, but grew rapidly through her website. Her local demand went up after participating in local craft fairs, so she decided to open a shop on Main Street.

Karen has one employee, Myrtle Cosner. She pays her monthly rent to a man named Brent Stratham.

With her different income streams and new expenses, she decided to purchase an online bookkeeping software to help her keep track of her books. Let's help her!! :)

The first thing we need to do is set up Karen's Chart of Accounts.

The Chart of Accounts is a list of all of the different categories that a transaction can fall under in the business.

Each business's chart of accounts looks slightly different, and is tailored to that business's specific needs.

Remember the accounting equation? Assets = Liabilities + Equity. We're going to use this layout to describe the chart of accounts, starting with the assets.

ASSETS

Karen's assets are all of the things that she owns in her business. Here is a list of her asset accounts:

-Checking Account 1234
-Savings Account 0000
-Cash on Hand
-Accounts Receivable (money owed to Karen)

LIABILITIES

Karen's liabilities are what she owes to other businesses/people. Here is a list of her liability accounts:

-Credit Card 4321
-Accounts Payable (money Karen owes for bills, etc.)

EQUITY

Karen's equity accounts are the value of what's left when you subtract her liabilities from her assets. Equity also includes the income, cost of goods sold, and expenses of the business, which I will point out separately.

-Opening Balance Equity (the balance of accounts when beginning record-keeping)
-Owner's Investment (of personal money into business)

-Owner's Pay (personal expenses from the business account also go here, like if you use the wrong card on accident)
-Retained Earnings (previous years' earnings)

Income Accounts

-Store Sales
-Online Sales

Cost of Goods Sold Accounts

-Cost of Goods Sold (COGS)

Expense Accounts

-Advertising
-Car and Truck expenses
-Contract labor
-Insurance
-Interest expense
-Legal and professional services
-Meals
-Office expenses
-Rent or lease
-Repairs and Maintenance
-Taxes and Licenses
-Travel
-Utilities
-Wages

A common bookkeeping question is the difference between Cost of Goods Sold and expenses. For Karen, her Cost of Goods Sold is everything she must purchase in order to make the QUILTS, such as material, needles, scissors, and batting. Her expenses are the purchases she must make in order to keep the BUSINESS running.

So, when you connect your bank accounts to the software and see each transaction come in, you're going to look at each one and decide which one of the accounts listed above that it needs to go in!

If you are unsure about a specific transaction, you can always create a separate expense account called Ask My Accountant. (Some software comes with this account included.)

You can also email me with any questions on this chapter or in your specific business, and I'll be happy to help! :)

Let's dive in and get some practice with Karen's October transactions!

4. Karen's October Transactions

Now that we know what Karen's Chart of Accounts looks like, we can organize all of her transactions into those categories.

Her **transaction list** consists of any time that money came in or out of her company.

For our example, we are organizing all of the transactions from her checking account.

As you may have noticed in Chapter 3, Karen DOES have a credit card. To make things simpler, we are pretending that she doesn't use her credit card anymore, she just needs to pay the rest of the balance off. If she did use her credit card, there would be a different transaction list for that card. The same is true if she had multiple cards or bank accounts--each one would be its own category in the chart of accounts, and each would have its own transaction list.

When Karen signs in to the software and connects her bank account, this is what she sees:

October Transactions: Checking Account 1234		
Description	Spent	Received
Material and Needles	45.28	
Signs Plus	57.61	
Groceries	116.34	
Brent Stratham	650.00	
Myrtle Cosner	415.59	
Social Media Ad	250.00	
Quilt Me One Too		1,469.25
Power and Light	89.45	
Transfer	1,200.00	
Office Pens and Paper	15.49	
Sewing Machines Plus	249.81	
Quilt Me One Too		984.26
POS		650.46
Discount Fabric	46.59	
Discount Batting	68.19	
Quilt Me One Too		2,016.49

Myrtle Cosner	415.59	
POS		1,269.16
Credit Card Payment	134.00	
Water Bros.	46.15	
Material and Needles	59.96	
Discount Fabric	289.16	
Discount Batting	349.19	
Hotel	256.76	
Vendor Booth	746.19	
The Best Restaurant	56.13	
Gas	34.19	
Quilt Me One Too		134.16
Deposit		1,486.49
POS		885.46
Discount Fabric	806.74	
Transfer	1,200.00	
Savings	750.00	

Let's help her get figure out what to do with all of these transactions!

I'm going to go through each transaction in October and label it, with a brief description of why I chose to put it in saidcategory:

October Transactions: Checking Account 1234			
Description	Spent	Received	Account
Material and Needles	45.28		COGS (She uses this to actually assemble the quilts)
Signs Plus	57.61		Advertising (Her company name on a sign is an advertisement for her company.)
Groceries	116.34		Owner's Pay (She accidentally used the wrong card at checkout.)
Brent Stratham	650.00		Rent or Lease (Brent is her Landlord.)
Myrtle Cosner	415.59		Wages (Myrtle is her employee.)
Social Media	250.00		Advertising

Ad			(An ad on social media is an advertisement for her company.)
Quilt Me One Too		1,469.25	Online Sales (This is her website name.)
Power and Light	89.45		Utilities (Electricity for her store.)
Transfer	1,200.00		Owner's Pay (She is transferring money to a personal account.)
Office Pens and Paper	15.49		Office Supplies (She purchased items for the store/her office.)
Sewing Machines Plus	249.81		COGS (She uses this to make the quilts.)
Quilt Me One Too		984.26	Online Sales

POS		650.46	Store Sales (This is her Point-of-Sale system in the store to capture payments.)
Discount Fabric	46.59		COGS (She uses this to make the quilts.)
Discount Batting	68.19		COGS (She uses this to make the quilts.)
Quilt Me One Too		2,016.49	Online Sales
Myrtle Cosner	415.59		Wages
POS		1,269.16	Store Sales
Credit Card Payment	134.00		Credit Card (She is trying to pay off the credit card balance.)
Water Bros.	46.15		Utilities (Water for the store.)
Material and Needles	59.96		COGS (She uses this

			to make the quilts.)
Discount Fabric	289.16		COGS (She uses this to make the quilts.)
Discount Batting	349.19		COGS (She uses this to make the quilts.)
Hotel	256.76		Travel (She is traveling for business.)
Vendor Booth	746.19		Advertisement (She has a booth set up with pamphlets about her business.)
The Best Restaurant	56.13		Meals (She ate out with Myrtle to discuss business ideas.)
Gas	34.19		Travel (She paid for fuel for her business trip.)

Quilt Me One Too		134.16	Online Sales
Deposit		1,486.49	Owner's Investment (She put her personal money into the business.)
POS		885.46	Store Sales
Discount Fabric	806.74		COGS (She uses this to make the quilts.)
Transfer	1,200.00		Owner's Pay
Savings	750.00		Savings 0000 (She is putting money away in a savings account to pay her taxes later.)
Total Change	**8,348.41**	**8,895.73**	**547.32**

Now that we've categorized everything, we can go to the "Reports" section in the software! There, you will find the Profit and Loss report and Balance Sheet. The following chapters will explain those two reports and how they can help your business.

5. THE PROFIT AND LOSS REPORT

You are going to LOVE THIS!

This is where you find out how much money you're making! Whoo hoo!! :)

Remember our Income, Cost of Goods Sold, and Expense accounts in our chart of accounts? Those are going to be featured here in order to get the month's net income!

The profit and loss starts and ends on specific dates (usually the first and last day of the month/year, but you can always customize it.)

Here is the layout of the **Profit and Loss** report: Income - Cost of Goods Sold = Gross Profit, then Gross Profit - Total Expenses = Net Income.

Let's do Karen's Profit and Loss report for October using the transactions we just classified. I simply took the total of all of the transactions in each category to get my final number. For example, Online Sales is 4,604.16 because of the four transactions she had in October= 1,469.25 + 984.26 + 2,016.49 + 134.16.

Profit and Loss October 1, 2021 - October 31, 2021	
Income	
Online Sales	4,604.16
Store Sales	2,805.08
Total Income	7,409.24
COST OF GOODS SOLD	
COGS	1,914.92
Total Cost of Goods Sold	1,914.92
Gross Profit	5,494.32
EXPENSES	
Advertising	1,053.80
Meals	56.13
Office expenses	15.49
Rent or Lease	650.00
Travel	290.95
Utilities	135.60
Wages	831.18
Total Expenses	3,033.15
NET INCOME	**2,461.17**

You might have noticed that the profit and loss report doesn't necessarily have ALL of our different expense categories in it. That's okay! Some months, you won't have any expenses in a certain category. If an expense category isn't mentioned here, then the balance in that account is zero.

Also, the profit and loss report ONLY includes income accounts, Cost of Goods Sold accounts, and expense accounts.

And there you have it! Wouldn't you love to see all of your income and expenses laid out like this so you know how much you're making each month? :)

6. THE BALANCE SHEET

After all of our work up to this point, the balance sheet is going to be a *breeze*!

The Balance Sheet shows you what the balances in your accounts are at a specific moment in time. The easiest part of this report is that it's set up *exactly like the accounting equation!* We know that guy by heart by now! :) Assets = Liabilities + Equity.

Below is an example of what Karen's balance sheet looks like *before* we started helping her. It records all of the information from the beginning of time to the date listed at the top (September 30, 2021.)

Balance Sheet As of September 30, 2021	
ASSETS	
Checking Account 1234	4,921.23

Savings Account 0000	10,468.24
Cash on Hand	550.00
Accounts Receivable	0.00
Total Assets	**$15,939.47**
LIABILITIES	
Credit Card	399.88
Accounts Payable	0.00
Total Liabilities	**$399.88**
EQUITY	
Opening Balance Equity	2,561.72
Owner's Investment	1,661.44
Owner's Pay	-5,260.15
Retained Earnings	10,520.30
Net Income	6,056.28
Total Equity	**$15,539.59**
Total Liabilities + Equity	**$15,939.47**

As you can see here, the Assets = Liabilities +Equity! It's all shown here as a beautiful report! :)

You may notice that there is an account on here that *isn't* in our chart of accounts--Net Income.

Net Income isn't an account on it's own. **Net Income** is the amount the business owner gets when they subtract their expenses from their income. The net income in this report will cover from January 1, 2021 to October 31, 2021. (The net income from all previous years gets lumped together in Retained Earnings.) Each month, the net income will change (brought over from the Profit and Loss report) until the end of the year, when it is moved to Retained Earnings as well. (Don't worry, the main bookkeeping softwares do this for you automatically.)

Let's pretend that we run the Balance Sheet for October 31, 2021 (after we have categorized all of Karen's transactions.) This is what would change, with explanations:

Balance Sheet As of October 31, 2021	
ASSETS	
Checking Account 1234	4,921.23 + 547.32 = 5,468.55 (We add the positive difference from the transaction list.)
Savings Account 0000	10,468.24 + 750 = 11,218.24 (We add the money she put in savings.)
Cash on Hand	550.00
Accounts Receivable	0.00
Total Assets	5,468.55 + 11,218.24 + 550 = **$17,236.79**

LIABILITIES	
Credit Card	399.88 - 134 = 265.88 (We subtract her credit card payment.)
Accounts Payable	0.00
Total Liabilities	**$265.88**
EQUITY	
Opening Balance Equity	2,561.72
Owner's Investment	1,661.44 + 1,486.49 = 3,147.93 (We add the personal money she put into the business.)
Owner's Pay	-5,260.15 - 1,200 - 1,200 - 116.34 = -7,776.49 (We subtract the two times she paid herself, and also when she bought groceries on accident.)
Retained Earnings	10,520.30
Net Income	6,056.28 + 2,461.17 = 8,517.45 (We add the Net Income from the Profit and Loss report.)
Total Equity	**2,561.72 + 3,147.93 +10,520.30 + 8,517.45 - 7776.49 = $16,970.91**
Total Liabilities + Equity	**265.88 + 16,970.91 = $17,236.79**

And there you have it! Now that you know how to do all of this stuff, it's time to try it out for yourself!

The next chapter will give you the opportunity to help Karen with her November transactions. If you are unsure of how to categorize something or where to put it, you can come back here to see how I did it, or jump ahead to the next chapter to peek at the answers.

Good luck! :)

7. Karen's November Transactions and Reports

Here's your chance to shine!! :)

Take the knowledge that you've gained so far and use it to classify each of Karen's transactions into the right category/account. The blank column on the right is for you to write your answers in.

November Transactions: Checking 1234			
Description	Spent	Received	Which account?
Material and Needles	62.75		
Groceries	25.49		
Brent Stratham	650.00		
Myrtle Cosner	415.59		

Social Media Ad	375.00		
Quilt Me One Too		1,294.65	
Power and Light	89.45		
Transfer	1,200.00		
Office Pens and Paper	24.16		
Sewing Machines Plus	284.72		
Quilt Me One Too		784.16	
POS		751.29	
Discount Fabric	52.49		
Discount Batting	72.96		
Quilt Me One Too		2,349.82	
Myrtle Cosner	415.59		
POS		1,531.49	
Water Bros.	46.15		
Material	62.82		

Discount Fabric	165.46		
Discount Batting	372.84		
Vendor Booth	746.19		
The Best Restaurant	42.49		
Quilt Me One Too		426.49	
Credit Card Payment	134.00		
POS		985.26	
Discount Fabric	814.72		
Transfer	1,200.00		
Savings	750.00		
Total change			

Now that you've got her transactions figured out, fill out her Profit and Loss report and Balance Sheet for November 2021.

(Remember, the Profit and Loss starts over fresh for November, but you'll need to take the balances in the October 31, 2021 Balance Sheet from Chapter 6 and *update* them with the new information above to reach your new balances for November 30, 2021.)

Profit and Loss November 1, 2021 - November 30, 2021	
Income	
Online Sales	
Store Sales	
Total Income	
COST OF GOODS SOLD	
COGS	
Total Cost of Goods Sold	
Gross Profit	
EXPENSES	
Advertising	
Meals	
Office expenses	
Rent or Lease	
Travel	
Utilities	
Wages	
Total Expenses	
NET INCOME	

Balance Sheet As of November 30, 2021	
ASSETS	
Checking Account 1234	
Savings Account 0000	
Cash on Hand	
Accounts Receivable	
Total Assets	
LIABILITIES	
Credit Card	
Accounts Payable	
Total Liabilities	
EQUITY	
Opening Balance Equity	
Owner's Investment	
Owner's Pay	
Retained Earnings	
Net Income	
Total Equity	
Total Liabilities + Equity	

8. Answer Key

Here are the answers to the transactions and reports in the previous chapter.

If you are unsure why you got one or more wrong, email me! :)

November Transactions: Checking 1234			
Description	Spent	Received	Which account?
Material and Needles	62.75		COGS
Groceries	25.49		Owner's Pay
Brent Stratham	650.00		Rent
Myrtle Cosner	415.59		Wages
Social Media Ad	375.00		Advertising

Quilt Me One Too		1294.65	Online Sales
Power and Light	89.45		Utilities
Transfer	1,200.00		Owner's Pay
Office Pens and Paper	24.16		Office Supplies
Sewing Machines Plus	284.72		COGS
Quilt Me One Too		784.16	Online Sales
POS		751.29	Store Sales
Discount Fabric	52.49		COGS
Discount Batting	72.96		COGS
Quilt Me One Too		2,349.82	Online Sales
Myrtle Cosner	415.59		Wages
POS		1,531.49	Store Sales
Water Bros.	46.15		Utilities
Material and Needles	62.82		COGS
Disc. Fabric	165.46		COGS

Discount Batting	372.84		COGS
Vendor Booth	746.19		Advertising
The Best Restaurant	42.49		Meals
Quilt Me One Too		426.49	Online Sales
Credit Card Payment	134.00		Credit Card
POS		985.26	Store Sales
Discount Fabric	814.72		COGS
Transfer	1,200.00		Owner's Pay
Savings	750.00		Savings
Total change	8,002.87	8,123.16	120.29

Profit and Loss November 1, 2021- November 30, 2021	
Income	
Online Sales	4,855.12
Store Sales	3,268.04
Total Income	**8,123.16**
COST OF GOODS SOLD	
COGS	1,888.76
Total Cost of Goods Sold	**1,888.76**
Gross Profit	**6,234.40**
EXPENSES	
Advertising	1,121.19
Meals	42.49
Office expenses	24.16
Rent or Lease	650.00
Utilities	135.60
Wages	831.18
Total Expenses	2,804.62
NET INCOME	**3,429.78**

Balance Sheet As of November 30, 2021	
ASSETS	
Checking Account 1234	5,588.84
Savings Account 0000	11,968.24
Cash on Hand	550.00
Accounts Receivable	0.00
Total Assets	**18,107.08**
LIABILITIES	
Credit Card	131.88
Accounts Payable	0.00
Total Liabilities	**$131.88**
EQUITY	
Opening Balance Equity	2,561.72
Owner's Investment	3,147.93
Owner's Pay	-10,201.98
Retained Earnings	10,520.30
Net Income	11,947.23
Total Equity	**17,975.20**
Total Liabilities + Equity	**18,107.08**

9. Records, Receipts, and Randoms*

*All of the following information is based on the current information I found at www.irs.gov in August 2021, when this book was updated. Tax laws change all the time, so be sure to rely on what the IRS website says, not on what is written here.

What form do I file for my business?

The type of business that you have determines the form that you file with the IRS. You can see the tax information for businesses here: https://www.irs.gov/businesses

In general, these are the forms that different businesses file based on type:

Individuals and Single LLCs	Form 1040, Schedule C
Partnerships	1065
S-Corps	1120-S
C-Corps	1120

What qualifies as a deduction?

The reason we are sorting our income and expenses into different categories is so we know how much we can deduct when it's time to file our taxes.

You can see a list of what all a business can deduct here: www.irs.gov/businesses/small-businesses-self-employed/deducting-business-expenses

Setting aside money for taxes/quarterly estimates

As a general rule, if you expect to owe more than $1,000, you need to pay quarterly estimates with the IRS.

The current due dates for the quarterly estimates are:
- April 15, 2021 (covering Jan. 1- March 31)
- June 15, 2021 (covering April 1- May 31)
- Sept. 15, 2021 (covering June 1- August 31)
- Jan. 18, 2022 (covering Sept. 1- Dec. 31)

To figure out *how* to make these payments, you can go to www.irs.gov/payments. Here, you can see your different payment options (such as a bank account, debit or credit card, etc.)

To figure out *how much* you should be paying, you can view this form here: www.irs.gov/pub/irs-pdf/f1040es.pdf. Here, you can view the worksheet that helps you figure out how much you owe based on your household income, tax bracket, etc.

What Kind of Records to Keep

You can see what records the IRS says to keep here: www.irs.gov/businesses/small-businesses-self-employed/what-kind-of-records-should-i-keep.

Some of the types of records you should keep are gross receipts, purchases, expenses, and receipts from buying and selling assets.

You should keep most records for at least three years. However, some records are supposed to be kept as long as 7 years, such as documents from claiming a bad-debt deduction. You can see the length of time that you're supposed to keep certain documents here: www.irs.gov/businesses/small-businesses-self-employed/how-long-should-i-keep-records.

When deciding what records to keep, make sure that you have itemized receipts. A receipt that says you spent $30 at Walmart isn't going to be enough. The IRS needs to see what items you bought that totaled $30.

Filing a 1099-MISC or 1099-NEC

If you are paying a person/business, and they are not on your payroll, you may need to file a 1099-MISC form for them.

A general rule is that you need to file a 1099-MISC for all people/businesses that you pay by check over the amount of $600.

HOWEVER, there are tons of nuances and specifics as to who requires one. You can read the instructions here: www.irs.gov/businesses/small-businesses-self-employed/am-i-required-to-file-a-form-1099-or-other-information-return

(There is a new form called the 1099-NEC. Be sure to double-check which one applies to your contactors and their situations.)

What if I have more questions?

You probably have more questions than I have answers in this chapter. Each person reading this will have a specific situation and wonder what to do about it.

First, there is A LOT of information on the IRS website. It is there to help out ALL business owners, not just accountants. Any time you have a question, you can go to their website and type it in the search bar. Chances are, other people have had that question as well, and so the IRS has answered it.

If not, please contact your bookkeeper or CPA. Like I said, every situation is different, and they can help you figure out the answer for YOU in your current situation! :)

10. BONUS CHAPTER: DEBITS AND CREDITS

This is a bonus chapter to help you better understand what's going on behind-the-scenes in the bookkeeping software.

Most people struggle with Debits and Credits because they think about them in the wrong way. Let's start off on the right foot:

Debit means left, and **Credit** means right.

That's it.

Neither is good or bad, neither means addition or subtraction.

Again, Debit means left and Credit means right.

The "T" Account

Debit	Credit

You see how the lines on the image look like the letter T? This is a T account.

Remember how I said that in double-entry bookkeeping, every time there is a transaction, two accounts will be affected? This is how. In every transaction, one account is debited, and one is credited.

Another important note is that **the debits must always equal the credits.**

Each account in the chart of accounts has a debit or credit balance. A cheat sheet is listed below:

Assets: Debit Balance

This includes checking accounts, savings accounts, cash on hand, and accounts receivable.

Liabilities: Credit Balance

This includes credit cards and accounts payable.

Equity: Credit Balance

This includes opening balance equity, owner's investment, retained earnings, and net income. However, owner's pay technically has a "Contra" credit balance, which makes it negative. Some people describe this as a debit balance.

Income: Credit Balance

This includes ALL of the different income accounts for the business.

Cost of Goods Sold and Expenses: Debit Balance

This includes all COGS accounts and all expense accounts.

When you want to **increase something** with a **debit balance**, you put it on the left side, or debit side, of the T account.

When you want to **decrease something** with a **debit balance**, you put it on the right side, or the credit side, of the T account.

When you want to **increase something** with a **credit balance**, you put it on the right side, or the credit side, of the T account.

When you want to **decrease something** with a **credit balance**, you put it on the left side, or debit side, of the T account.

Account	Normal Balance	To Increase	To Decrease
Assets	Debit	Debit	Credit
Liabilities	Credit	Credit	Debit
Equity	Credit	Credit	Debit
Income	Credit	Credit	Debit
COGS and Expenses	Debit	Debit	Credit

Now that we've got that covered, let's see how this actually works!

Let's go through some of Karen's transactions in October to see this work in action!

Example 1 - Asset to Asset

Karen transferred 750.00 to her Savings account. This affects her checking account (because that's where the money came from) and her Savings account (because that's where the money is going.)

Her checking account has a debit balance, so we want to credit it to decrease it, because money is being taken out of the account.

Her Savings account has a debit balance, so we want to debit it to increase it, because money is going into that account.

Debit	Credit
Savings 750.00	Checking 750.00

Example 2 - Asset to Liability

Karen paid 134.00 toward her credit card. This affects her checking account (because that's where the money came from) and her Credit Card account (because that's where the money is going.)

Her checking account has a debit balance, so we want to credit it to decrease it, because money is being taken out of the account.

Her Credit Card account has a credit balance, so we want to debit it to decrease it, because we are trying to pay off that balance.

Debit	Credit
Credit Card 134.00	Checking 134.00

Example 3 - Equity to Asset

Karen put 1,486.49 of her personal money into the business. This affects her checking account (because that's where the money is going) and Owner's Investment (because that's where the money came from.)

Her checking account has a debit balance, so we want to debit it to increase it, because money is being added to the account.

Her Owner's Investment account has a credit balance, so we want to credit it to increase it, because the overall amount of money she has added to the company is increasing.

Debit	Credit
Checking 1,486.49	Owner's Investment 1,486.49

Example 4- Asset to Equity

Karen transferred 1,200.00 to Owner's Pay. This affects her checking account (because that's where the money came from) and her Owner's Pay account (because that's where we are classifying it.)

Her checking account has a debit balance, so we want to credit it to decrease it, because money is being taken out of the account.

Her Owner's Pay account has a negative credit (or debit) balance, so we want to debit it to increase it, because we want the amount to become more negative.

Debit	Credit
Owner's Pay 1,200.00	Checking 1,200.00

Example 5- Income to Asset

Karen received 1,469.25 for quilts from her website. This affects her checking account (because that's where the money is going) and her Online Sales account (because that's where we are classifying it.)

Her checking account has a debit balance, so we want to debit it to increase it, because money is being added to the account.

Her Online Sales account has a credit balance, so we want to credit it to increase it, because the amount she has made in Online Sales is increasing.

Debit	Credit
Checking 1,469.25	Online Sales 1,469.25

Example 6- Asset to COGS

Karen purchased material and needles for 45.28. This affects her checking account (because that's where the money came from) and her COGS account (because that's where we are classifying it.)

Her checking account has a debit balance, so we want to credit it to decrease it, because money is leaving the account.

Her COGS account has a debit balance, so we want to debit it to increase it, because the amount she spent on COGS is increasing.

Debit	Credit
COGS 45.28	Checking 45.28

Example 7- Asset to Expense

Karen paid Brent Stratham 650.00 for rent. This affects her checking account (because that's where the money came from) and her Rent expense account (because that's where we are classifying it.)

Her checking account has a debit balance, so we want to credit it to decrease it, because money is being taken out of the account.

Her Rent expense account has a debit balance, so we want to debit it to increase it, because the amount she has spent on rent is increasing.

Debit	Credit
Rent 650.00	Checking 650.00

The good part about this is that if you are using software to keep your books, half of this is happening behind the scenes. The only time I use this in my bookkeeping is when I have to enter something manually, which I do by doing a Journal Entry.

A **Journal Entry** is just like the T accounts above. You pick which accounts you want to be affected, decide which one needs to be debited and which one needs to be credited, and by how much. The debits must always equal the credits.

There it is! That's your behind-the-scenes look at debits and credits! :)

A great resource for how to understand this better is AccountingCoach.com. They have a lot of accurate, free resources there for students, small businesses, and bookkeepers.

valerie@profitmeadow.com

About Valerie Johnston (ME!)

I'm a Christian, wife, mother, and bookkeeper, making a living doing what I love!! :)

I love bookkeeping and just finished my first handmade quilt, which gave me the inspiration for Karen! :)

Some people may think that it's crazy for me to explain exactly what I do in a book and sell it to my potential clients, but I think they're wrong.

Equipping you with the tools for success is not a threat to me or my job. In fact, if you do this stuff well, you'll beable to see how much money you're making each month AND the equity you have in your business. If you do that, you'll be able to scale your business and actually afford to hire someone like me when your plate is too full of other management responsibilities (like filling all of those orders!)

I want to teach you. I want you to learn. I want you to succeed.

That's why I started Profit Meadow Bookkeeping in the first place! I want to help you on your way to success!

If you want to get in touch with me to ask any questions about the book, to schedule a free consultation, or to simply tell me I'm crazy and I've alleviated your need for a bookkeeper entirely, here are the different ways that you can do that! :)

Email: valerie@profitmeadow.com
Website: www.profitmeadow.com
Text: 404-692-3553
LinkedIn: www.linkedin.com/in/valerie-johnston-92926b140/
Facebook: https://www.facebook.com/profitmeadowbookkeeping/
Instagram: https://www.instagram.com/profitmeadowbookkeeping/

Made in the USA
Middletown, DE
17 August 2022

71495349R00035